Young Carson

Rachel Carson was born in Pennsylvania in 1907. She lived in a small town called Springdale. When she was young, she loved to explore the woods near her house. She listened to birds and watched insects.

Carson also loved the water. She lived close to a large river called the Allegheny, but her dream was to see the ocean. Springdale was far from the closest ocean, the Atlantic. Carson hoped to see the ocean one day.

Springdale is far from the ocean.

Carson had other interests, too. She loved to read and write. She enjoyed reading stories from a children's magazine. When Carson was ten, she wrote a story and sent it to a magazine. It was about a pilot fighting in a war.

To her surprise, the magazine printed the story! Carson was excited about seeing her story in the magazine, so she wrote more stories. She decided she would become a writer when she grew up.

Young Carson loved to write stories.

Going to Coll

Carson was a good high school student and first in her class. She wanted to go to college to learn to be a better writer. She decided to go to a college in nearby Pittsburgh.

College was expensive. Carson's parents wanted to help. They sold some of their farmland to pay for part of the cost of college. They wanted Carson to fulfill her dreams.

Carson saw that Pittsburgh was very different from Springdale. In the 1920s, Pittsburgh was a **polluted** city. Pittsburgh had many steel mills. Because the steel mills burned coal to make steel, the air was black and smoky.

In college, Carson studied to become a writer. She took English classes. She also worked for the college newspaper and wrote stories for a college magazine. Although she had not seen the ocean, many of her stories were about the sea.

Pittsburgh in the early 1900s

Carson studied hard in college.

Carson took a class in biology, the study of plants and animals. She loved it! The class went on field trips, which reminded Carson of her childhood when she explored the woods.

Carson made a big decision. She switched her focus at school from English to science. She still loved to write. Yet she wanted to learn more about nature. She wanted to become a scientist.

After she graduated college in 1929, Carson went home. Things had changed. The rivers were brown and dirty. The air was also polluted. Local power plants were to blame for the pollution. The plants burned coal and released smoke into the air. They dumped waste into the rivers.

Carson never forgot what she saw in Pittsburgh or her hometown. One day her work would teach others about the dangers of pollution.

When cities grow, pollution can worsen.

Carson studied marine life at Woods Hole, Massachusetts.

Becoming a Scientist

While she was home, Carson told her family some good news. She had been accepted into a study program with other scientists. It was in Massachusetts, on the Atlantic Ocean.

Carson spent several weeks by the ocean, learning about **marine** animals. She could smell the salt water and hear the waves. Her childhood dream had come true.

Next, Carson got a job with the United States government. She wrote stories for a radio show. The show taught listeners about ocean life. Carson was happy. Her work used her two favorite things—writing and science.

Carson also wrote newspaper articles about nature. Readers liked the beautiful descriptions of ocean life. One of her articles caught the attention of a book publisher. They asked Carson to write a book about the sea.

Carson wrote books about sea animals such as this sandpiper.

Carson's book was called *Under the Sea Wind*. It was about the daily lives of ocean animals. The characters included a sandpiper, a fish, and an eel. The animals had lots of adventures. They traveled far and met lots of other animals.

Carson wrote two more books about the sea. They were big sellers. Carson was now a famous, successful author.

Farmers sometimes use planes to spray pesticides on crops.

Dangerous Chemicals

In the 1950s, Carson found a new topic to write about—**pesticides**. Pesticides are chemicals used to kill insects. Many farmers sprayed pesticides on their crops.

One of Carson's friends told her about finding many dead birds near her home. Pesticides had recently been sprayed nearby. Could the two events be connected? Carson decided to find out.

Carson did research about pesticides. She talked to experts. She found that pesticides were harmful to humans, animals, and water.

Animals that ate plants sprayed with pesticides could get sick. People could also get sick if they ate these plants or animals. Sometimes pesticides got into water. This water would be dangerous for people and animals. The chemicals could even cause people and animals to die.

In 1962 Carson published her most famous book, *Silent Spring*. The book warned people about the dangers of pesticides.

President John Kennedy heard about Carson's book. He ordered a study of pesticides. The government took action. Thanks to Carson's book, the use of many pesticides was limited. Some pesticides were even **banned**.

Carson died in 1964, but her words are still important today. She was one of the first **environmentalists**. She taught people about the importance of taking care of the environment. Today there are many laws that protect our air, water, and wildlife.

Glossary

ban to forbid the use of something

environmentalist a person concerned about protecting the air, soil, and water around us

marine having to do with the sea

pesticide a chemical mixture used to destroy insect pests

pollute to make a thing or a place dirty by adding harmful material

Scientist and Writer

Many scientists study nature and write about what they see. Rachel Carson was a scientist who loved to write. She wrote books about life in the ocean. But her most famous book is about protecting the environment. Carson's book made people understand that the environment was in great danger.

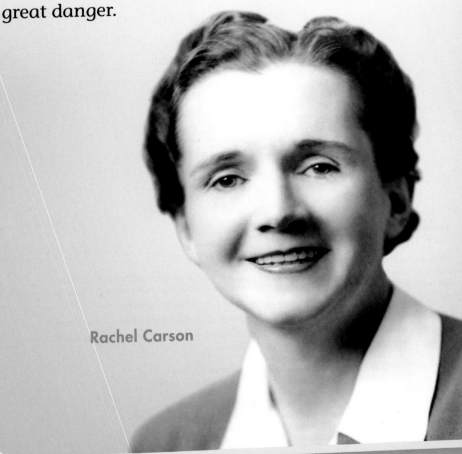

Rachel Carson

Rachel
Carson
Friend of Land and Sea

Darleen Ramos

Boston, Massachusetts
Chandler, Arizona
Glenview, Illinois
Upper Saddle River, New Jersey

Illustrations
Opener, 1, 4, 5, 7, 9, 10, 12, 14, 15 Meryl Treatner; 3 Joe LeMonnier.

Photographs
Every effort has been made to secure permission and provide appropriate credit for photographic material. The publisher deeply regrets any omission and pledges to correct errors called to its attention in subsequent editions.

Unless otherwise acknowledged, all photographs are the property of Pearson Education, Inc.

Photo locators denoted as follows: Top (T), Center (C), Bottom (B), Left (L), Right (R), Background (Bkgd)

2 U.S. Fish and Wildlife Service; 6 Library of Congress; 8 Jupiterimages/Thinkstock; 11 Photos to Go/Photolibrary; 13 (Inset) Comstock/Thinkstock.

ISBN-13: 978-0-328-67600-2
ISBN-10: 0-328-67600-4

2 3 4 5 6   V0FL   16 15 14 13 12